T0164980

Handbag Meditations

Chill out on the run

Women

Alison Nancye

BALBOA.
PRESS
A DIVISION OF HAY HOUSE

Balboa Press books may be ordered through booksellers or by contacting:

Balboa Press
A Division of Hay House
1663 Liberty Drive
Bloomington, IN 47403
www.balboapress.com.au
1-(877) 407-4847

ISBN: 978-1-4525-0796-5 (sc)
ISBN: 978-1-4525-0797-2 (e)

Printed in the United States of America

Balboa Press rev. date: 11/06/2012

For more resources:
www.alisonnancye.com
PO Box 88
Waverley NSW 2024
Sydney, Australia
info@thelifekitchen.com

also by alison nancye

non fiction
Recipes for Everyday Life
Planning a Career Change

fiction (adult)
Note to Self

fiction (children)
The Wisdom Office

"Peace. It does not
mean to be in a
place where there is
no noise, trouble or
hard work. It means
to be in the midst
of those things and
still be calm in
your heart".

Unknown

contents

meditation

I have been meditating for over 15 years. Put simply, I'm a better person when I meditate! But my healthy habits didn't begin then. I can trace it all the way back to my childhood.

My mum had me eating spoonfuls of molasses on a regular basis (disgusting!) as well as shopping for other strange and wonderful goodies at the health food store WAY before it became trendy! To top it off, mum woke me at the crack of dawn each day to tag along during her morning jog and swim at Bondi Beach.

I did NOT remotely value this dedication to my health back then, but you can guarantee I value it now! These lifestyle habits from an early age have well and truly set up the foundation for my life in the pursuit of happiness through healthy habits (on the inside and out!).

Finding meditation was the beginning to finding myself. My world (inner and outer) is all the better for meditating on a regular basis.

background

I use meditation most days. To de-stress, get focused,
when I'm unwell or tired, to connect with my dreams,
pursue my goals, and make decisions using my intuition.
Guess what . . . I also use it when writing my books
(including this one!).

Throughout my journey with meditation I have found that
it's more the *regular* practise of meditation that serves
me best. There are so many rituals I have written over the
years for myself, my children, husband, clients, friends, and
workshop participants, that I wanted to create a resource
of accessible meditations for anyone wanting to meditate
any time of the day.

When people ask me how I accomplish all the things I do
in the time frame that I do, yet still seem chilled, happy and
positive, my answer every single time is . . . *"I meditate!"*

So much peace, love, success, creativity, abundance,
fulfilment, pleasure and vitality happens when you use
meditation in your everyday life, that it pretty much
becomes a way of life.

I am thrilled to be sharing my meditation rituals with you
in this **HANDBAG MEDITATIONS for WOMEN** book.
Enjoy!

acknowledgments

To my gorgeous friend and creative collaborator Saffrine Nydegger, you ROCK! Thankyou! I had such a great ride being supported by you to get this series of meditation books created. **Exhale!**

To Therese Waters, I love brainstorming with you on our books. Thankyou for all your encouragement and guidance with this meditation book. **Focus!**

To Miriam Tassone, my best friend and soul sister. You are with me on every great journey I make in life. As ever, thankyou! **Manifest!**

special thanks

To my mum Patricia Ferris, thankyou for enforcing the value of being healthy from childhood and beyond. **Gratitude!**

To my husband Francesco Biffone and our gorgeous children Bellina and Benicio. Thankyou for sharing my dreams with me and creating an amazing life together. Amore always. **Love!**

"Meditation is the
window to your soul
and the doorway to
your heart."

Alison Nancye

During the time I wrote this book, I was also editing and releasing my first novel "NOTE TO SELF", while collaborating on a series of children's books titled "UMBRELLA GIRLS".

To up the ante (as we women do!), I was maintaining regular freelance work and actively involved in my children's school, including editor of a special edition school magazine.

I was enjoying a healthy and happy connection with my community of friends, along with spending fun, loving and vibrant times with my husband and kids.

Oh . . . and I didn't have a cleaner or a nanny (one day!), or a relative remotely closer than interstate or overseas to help with my kids at a moment's notice (working on the folks!). I am not telling you this to say, hey look at me I'm fabulous! I am sharing my life in a nutshell with you to highlight the power of meditation and what it can bring to your life overall.

When you meditate, you can actually achieve a lot in life in a really balanced and enjoyable way. I'm not suggesting you jam pack your life so it's bursting at the seams, more encouraging you to pack your life full of all the things you love.

handbag meditations

Life should be full of all the things you love to experience and do. Regular meditation, even mini doses, can help you to feel more focused, energised, centred, fulfilled, compassionate and creative, while living your life to the fullest every day.

The days I *do* meditate go SO much better than the days I *don't*.

I really do encourage you to try this regular meditation experiment for yourself.

Use these **HANDBAG MEDITATIONS** as a tool to give you at least a few minutes each day to breathe, be still, and just do . . . (or not do) whatever you would love in that moment.

Try all of the meditations in this book and use them whenever you can. Like anything, the more you practise, the easier it becomes.

HANDBAG MEDITATIONS for WOMEN is part of a series of books. There is a **HANDBAG MEDITATIONS** book for girls, teens, mums and grandmas too.

"Daydreaming is a
great place to begin
everyday realities."

Alison Nancye

For busy women on the go, meditation rituals are more often needed when you are running around during the day, than when you first wake up in the morning.

While it's beneficial to meditate each morning and night (please do! I have included meditations in this book for you), it's often right in those moments, when you are *literally* living life, when you need meditation most.

When things turn pear-shaped, when someone says or does something that upsets you, or when overloaded becomes an understatement, *that's* the time to use this book.

Dive into your handbag and retrieve your **HANDBAG MEDITATIONS for WOMEN** book and use it—*literally*!

handbag meditations

Use the meditations in this book while waiting for a bus, train or plane, during a meeting, before a date, in between tasks, or simply when you want to relax and dream.

It doesn't take much time to regroup, get focused, feel calmer and more centred using a powerful mini meditation ritual.

So ladies, keep this book in your handbag at all times, along with your phone, keys, wallet, lip gloss, sunscreen and other daily essentials.

HANDBAG MEDITATIONS for WOMEN is that essential accessory designed to help you fully function each day!

Happy Meditating!

There are so many definitions on meditation that I almost didn't want to include one in this book. But if you are new to meditation, you will probably want one, so here goes . . .

In the context of *this* book specifically, meditation is designed to assist busy women with quick ways to chill out, de-stress, regroup and take time to stop and breathe.

Meditation is the ability to take the time for yourself to be quiet, still and free from thought or focus on a single thought.

It is the experience of being fully present and connected to both your everyday-self and your higher-self to become one-self.

meditation

Now . . . having said all of that, once you get into your *own* rhythm with meditation, *you* will create your own personal definition of what meditation is—and you should!

The definition of meditation often defines *what* you need or want meditation for most at the time you are using it.

But no matter *when* you use meditation or *why* you use it, meditation is an incredibly powerful and profound tool that can be used from everything to quieten your mind, to manifesting your wildest dreams come true.

Have fun exploring your own pursuit of what meditation means to you.

My own experience of meditating tells me that it is *your own* experience of meditating that will advise you why and when meditation is beneficial.

I have started a list of meditation benefits and encourage you to use the lines provided to discover *your own* benefits of meditating too.

1. Increased energy
2. Improved clarity
3. Creativity and problem solving
4. Improved health and beauty
5. Enhanced memory
6. Stress relief and pain management
7. Greater compassion and understanding of others
8. Goal setting and life direction
9. Mind de-clutter and letting go
10. Relaxing, calming and soothing
11. Connect with your true nature
12. Recognise your innate gifts

meditating

_____

_____

_____

_____

_____

_____

_____

_____

_____

_____

_____

create

believe

receive

dream

achieve

Alison Nancye

breathe

focus

present

be

now

There are many tools you can use to give your meditation rituals and experiences that extra little touch. It is completely up to you *when* and *if* you want to use those tools to enhance your mood and mindset while meditating.

My general feeling is, if it *feels* good, it *is* good, so go for it!

However, if you feel your meditation experience is becoming more about the added extras than the actual *experience* of meditating, perhaps bring things back to basics for a while.

candles

Scented candles and incense sticks are a wonderful way to ignite the senses and create a specific mood for your meditation space.

music

Listening to inspiring and relaxing music, as well as instructor led meditation tracks, can be helpful to set the tone and guide you through your meditation experience.

pillow

A scented eye pillow will allow your eyes to rest and help you to let go and focus on your breath when meditating.

meditation experience

oils
Dab essential oil on your wrists or burn it in an oil burner to evoke a certain emotion or feeling while meditating. Vary the oils depending on your desired outcome.

sprays
There is such a diverse range of delicious face sprays you can purchase or make up yourself. Hydrating mists are fantastic for an instant hit to help all of the senses come alive in preparation for meditating.

tactile
Holding something in your hand can tell your body and mind you are in meditation mode. Prayer beads or a mood rock can be useful if you like tactile tools.

visual
Having artwork or a symbolic statue that makes you feel good when you look at it, can be a great tool to keep in view and set your mindset before and during meditation.

when to meditate

No matter whether you have or haven't meditated before, you should be able to master all of the meditations in this book.

They are designed to be easy to follow, effortless to use and enjoyable to experience. I have purposely kept these meditations simple, straightforward and specific in instruction. After all, meditation should bring ease to your life, not struggle!

Use the meditation steps in this book to guide you to that meditative space and state you so desire. Then spend as little or as much time during each meditation ritual, depending on how much time you have and how you are feeling on the day.

There will be days when some meditations in this book will be more appropriate than others. So choose the meditation you require most on the day you need it most.

Don't limit your meditation experience to just one or two rituals in this book. Try them all and use them all at various times in your life. Literally reach into your handbag and pull this meditation handbook out every day or as often as you can each week. Even if you only have a few minutes to spare, use the **HANDBAG MEDITATIONS for WOMEN** book to guide you to that place of inner peace, happiness, clarity and calm.

"When in
doubt, breathe."

Alison Nancye

choosing which

I use a variety of meditations depending on what I want to create, achieve, receive and experience. When I am not feeling my best, meditation is often the last thing I feel like doing. But every time I do it, I always feel SO much better afterwards.

For those days when you get in to a funk and everything becomes that little bit too hard, use the **Walking Release** meditation. When you don't have much time but want to start your day centred, use the **Happy Day** meditation.

Use the **Belly Breath** meditation either with your eyes opened or closed. It will relax you in seconds. It's as if it tells your body, to tell your mind, to tell your emotions, to calm down!

The **Day Dreaming** meditation is a fun way to connect with your dreams and big picture goals each year. You can also use it as a tool to inspire and focus you each week and month. It is such a great meditation ritual to give you clarity and direction in life.

The **Bathtime Bliss** meditation is fabulous for giving yourself some decadent, indulgent me time. Whilst the **Shower Cleanse** meditation is a great ritual that takes only a few minutes to let go of your day.

Use the **Be Grateful** meditation as often as you can. It's a very powerful tool to manifest a positive mindset *and* reality. The **Be Present** meditation will help you to feel more centred and connected as one in body, mind and spirit.

meditation to use

The **Ocean Gazing** meditation is a simple way to relax during an eyes open meditation. Whilst the **Do Nothing** meditation is a powerful way to close your eyes, and switch off from life and all that goes with it.

Use the **Birthday Wishes** meditation to manifest your dreams for the year ahead. The **Dream Date** meditation will help you to harness that goddess within to radiate out for your special occasion dates.

The **Conflict Clear** meditation is a great way to let go of negative emotions you may be holding on to as a result of conflict. Whilst the **Load Unload** meditation will guide you to literally let go of the overload in your life.

Use the **Healthy Healing** meditation when you are feeling unwell and the **Power On** meditation when there is too much to do and not enough hours in the day.

The **Mini Break** meditation is designed to give you regular short burst breaks throughout your workday. The **Intention List** meditation will help you to get clear about how you really want to spend your time each day.

The **Life Purpose** meditation will connect you to your innate talents and passions. The **Mind Unwind** meditation will help you clear your head and prepare for a restful night's sleep.

"There are many things we are good at, but what is it that truly makes you feel good."

Alison Nancye

bathtime bliss

Just thinking about having a bath can instantly start to relax you. Imagine how wonderful you will feel after you have *literally* languidly lay in your bathtub for as long as your mind, body and soul so desires.

Meditating on a flickering flame as you relax in a scented bath is a soothing and effortless way to de-clutter your mind, de-stress and let go of your day. It can also help to prepare you for a restful night's sleep.

Tip!
Add salt to your bath to release any toxic thoughts and unwanted feelings that may be running through your body and mind.

languid bathtime
lazing

Alison Nancye

meditation

1. Run a warm bath. Add any desired oils or salts.
2. Burn one bright candle, positioning it where you can easily see it from your bathtub.
3. Turn off the lights.
4. As you enter the bath, make a commitment to deeply relax, unwind, free your mind and literally let go.
5. As you relax in your warm scented bath, turn your attention now to the flickering flame of the candle.
6. With your eyes open, gently gaze at the flame and allow your breath to rise and fall in its own natural time and way.
7. Use the flickering flame of the candle as a visual tool at various intervals to let go of any thoughts that may be racing around in your mind.
8. Stay in the bath as long as you need and desire to gently unwind.

be grateful

As the theory goes, the more grateful you are, the more you have to be grateful for.

Easier said than done when life throws a chaotic day, week, month and heaven forbid . . . year at you!

But no matter what you've got going on in life, you can guarantee, some other fabulous woman half way across the world has got it all going on too.

Use the *'Be Grateful Meditation'* to switch your thoughts to positive ones and manifest a positive reality as a result.

You can use this ritual, any time, any where, and any how. Sitting, standing, showering, eyes opened or eyes closed.

create a grateful
reality

Alison Nancye

meditation

1. Choose one thing in your life that you are grateful for—anything! Focus on that now. Breathe in that thought.

2. Now say "THANKYOU FOR . . ." and name the thing you are grateful for (either out loud or to yourself).

3. Allow your mind to drift off to something else you are grateful for now—anything! It could be a lesson learned, seeing a baby smile, a gift someone gave you, a kind word said, your health, a windfall, or helpful shopkeeper. You choose.

4. Say "THANKYOU FOR . . ." and name the new thing you are grateful for.

5. Keep going until you feel complete. It could be one minute, several minutes or maybe more. Some days you will feel more grateful than others. Go with what feels right on the day.

be present

In the increasingly busy world we all live, women's workloads and to-do lists are getting fuller (and dare I say . . . out of control!). The amount of tasks, people and responsibilities we juggle on any given day, it's amazing we don't drop things, bump into things, forget things, lose things more often (well . . . more often than we already do!)

But if you are present, *truly* present and devote yourself to being more present each day, you will not only have more successful, brilliant and enjoyable days (and nights!), but you will also REMEMBER them as well!

Here's a quick way to switch from *off* to *on* each day.

switch from off to on

meditation

1. Sit in a chair or comfortable position and ensure you are free from distractions.
2. Gently close your eyes and turn your attention to your breath. Notice the natural rise and fall of your belly. There is no need to change your breathing in any way, simply observe your breath.
3. Notice any sounds you may hear. Noises close by or in the distance. Simply observe those sounds. Acknowledge any thoughts or feelings you may have. Now simply let go.
4. Let go of the thoughts. Let go of the feelings. Let go of the noise.
5. Be free to focus just on your breath.
6. Choose to be present today with others, with your work, with your family, with your environment, and with YOURSELF!
7. Say now, either out loud or to yourself three times, "I AM PRESENT TODAY IN EVERY WAY."
8. When you feel ready, gently open your eyes and slowly embrace your day.

belly breath

One of the first things we forget to do when we are stressed is BREATHE! Yet simply turning your attention *away* from the stress and *to* the breath, will calm you in seconds.

The *'Belly Breath Meditation'* is an effortless way to de-stress, focus, and take time out from your busy life. It is an incredibly powerful tool to harness your energy and centre yourself.

Tip!
You can do the *'Belly Breath Meditation'* with your eyes opened or closed. You can also use it when you are in the company of others.

take time out to
breathe

Alison Nancye

meditation

1. Choose a quiet place to meditate and ensure you are free from distractions.
2. Sit comfortably, gently close your eyes and turn your attention to your breath.
3. Notice the natural rise and fall of your belly.
4. There is no need to change your breathing in any way, simply observe your breath.
5. As you continue to observe your belly and the natural rhythms of your breath, you will start to feel more centred, grounded and relaxed overall.
6. Stay focused on your breath as long you like. A few seconds, a few minutes, whatever you need.
7. When you feel ready, gently open your eyes and return to your day.

birthday wishes

Birthdays are a wonderful time to set an intention to manifest new dreams to look forward to. But who said we could only have one wish at cake time!

Use the *'Birthday Wishes Meditation'* to dream on, create and manifest your heartfelt dreams and desires for the year ahead.

Tip!
Remember to celebrate your dreams!

manifest your heart's
desires

meditation

1. In a comfortable, quiet spot, sit down and close your eyes. Allow yourself to feel more relaxed with each new breath in and out.
2. Imagine a big delicious birthday cake being placed in front of you (forget about the calorie counting for today!).
3. As you gaze at your birthday cake, start to allow wishes you would love to come true throughout the year ahead to form in your imagination now. Spend as long as you like connecting to these dreams and desires.
4. Now imagine elegant birthday candles resting beside your cake. Each candle represents a dream you would love to come true before your next birthday.
5. Slowly place each dream candle on your cake. Take a moment to focus on each candle and connect to the individual dream it represents.
6. Once you have placed all your birthday dreams on your cake, take a generous moment to breathe in and imagine your life with all of those dreams coming true. Then when you feel ready, imagine gently blowing out all of the candles together. Sending your wishes out to the universe to come true over the coming year ahead. Then open your eyes.
7. Make a note of your dreams in your favourite journal. Use these notes and visual cues to inspire you to reconnect with your birthday dreams. Take steps towards these dreams as often as you like over the year ahead.

conflict clear

Having an incident with a colleague, boss, customer, client, loved one, family member or friend, can cause havoc in your life.

Some of us are better than others at dealing with conflict, letting it go and moving on after the conflict has occurred. But all of us have the opportunity to get better at handling and moving on from conflict more swiftly through practise.

Try this meditation next time someone or something really gets on your nerves, upsets you or sends you over the edge!

exhale and let it go

meditation

1. Immediately or soon after the conflict has occurred, head to the nearest bathroom or outside in the fresh air if you can.
2. Exhale. Literally, loudly and physically exhale.
3. Now breathe in and breathe out 10 times loudly, becoming more centred and focused on your breath each time.
4. For the next series of 10 breaths in and out, during the out breath, drag your hand and fingers all the way down each arm from your shoulders right through to your fingertips and beyond, into the air in front of you.
5. Finish by gently shaking your hands out and flicking your fingertips out to the air.
6. Later that day or as soon as you can, take a swim in the ocean or have a relaxing saltwater bath. The salt will help to further release any toxic feelings you may be carrying energetically or emotionally as a result of the conflict.

day dreaming

Dreaming on your dreams is a wonderful way to de-stress, feel relaxed, increase energy levels and get clear about what you really want from life.

When we are continuously busy and ingrained in the day to day, we often forget that taking time out to dream, is just as important as taking the time to move through the daily to do list.

We all feel better having things to look forward to. Sometimes the day dreaming about things on the horizon will give you just as much happiness as fulfilling that dream for real (well almost!). When we put ourselves in to a happy and positive state of mind using meditation, it has a significant impact on our happiness levels, right here right now.

You can use the *'Day Dreaming Meditation'* any time in your day, week or year.

Tip!
You can do this meditation exercise whenever you would like to add to your dreams or create new dreams to work towards. You can also use this exercise to focus on a specific area of your life. For example career, relationships, family, finances, health, travel, home, etc.

dream on your dreams

meditation

1. Set an intention for the timeframe for your dreams (3 months, 6 months, 1 year, 2 years?). Have a paper and pen nearby.

2. Focus on your breath. Acknowledge any thoughts or feelings you may have and let them go on each out breath.

3. Imagine yourself in a place of nature now anywhere in the world. Take in the sights, smells, and sounds in this place of nature.

4. Now imagine yourself as a little girl in that picture of nature. An image from your childhood completely innocent and carefree.

5. Now imagine the adult you, holding hands with the little girl you and together looking up to a glorious blue sky above. The sun is shining down and warming you both. Imagine now as you look up in the sky, the vision for your life and dreams ahead for the desired timeframe taking place right now. Whatever you get; words, a feeling, an image, a scene taking place, it's all meaningful. Breathe and take it all in.

6. When you feel ready, open your eyes and write your dreams on your notepaper. It may be one thing or many things. Whatever it is, make notes.

7. Use your notes to inspire and direct you to your dreams. Allow these fresh new insights to give you clarity of the things you would love to look forward to in life and manifest for real. Let these dreams be a guide to taking steps towards a life you truly love.

do nothing

Feel like there is always something to do?

Doing nothing is something women worldwide should practise whenever we can. I am still practising the art of nothingness. That's why I have included it in this book!

Giving yourself the opportunity to literally *do nothing* is an art, a skill, and a *massive* feat for many. But with practise, you will begin to crave doing nothing because of the benefits it will begin to bring to your life overall.

Tip!
If you want to do this meditation before going to sleep, go for it!

the art of nothingness

meditation

1. Set an intention for how long you want to spend meditating. Turn your phone on silent (or if you're really brave, switch it off altogether!). Dim the lights or turn them off completely.

2. Lie down and ensure you feel comfortable and warm. If you have an eye pillow, place it over your closed eyes. Let your arms rest by your sides.

3. You are now going to switch off your body from head to toe. Imagine there is a light switch that you are literally switching off at each point. Start at your head, move through to your eyes, nose and ears. Continue all the way down through your body finishing at your toes. Choose one final off switch for your entire body now.

4. Breathe in the blackness. The darkness. The nothingness. Relax. Stay in this meditative state as long as you desire.

5. When you feel complete, switch the lights back on. This time start at your toes and move all the way back up to the top of your head. Turn each light switch back on at various intervals in your body. Then choose one final on switch for your entire body.

6. Slowly remove your eye pillow. Wriggle your fingers and toes. Gently stretch and sit up. When you feel ready, slowly reconnect with your day.

dream date

I've had my fair share of successful and not so successful dates during my dating days! The only difference between the two had nothing to do with the *date* and everything to do with *me*.

The *'Dream Date Meditation'* will help you embrace the goddess within and be more like your true self on your desired date, no matter whom you are dating.

Tip!
If your delicious date turns into a disaster date, head to the bathroom, regroup and do the *'Belly Breath Meditation.'*

ooze the goddess within

Alison Nancye

meditation

1. Sit comfortably, close your eyes and allow your breath to rise and fall in its own natural way.

2. Imagine yourself on a holiday now anywhere in the world, having the time of your life. You may be relaxing, dancing, eating, chilling, swimming, sightseeing, daydreaming. Whatever it is, just observe yourself on this holiday feeling fabulous!

3. Now imagine an image of you on this holiday dressed up and looking stunning. Connect to this image of you utterly in your element, looking and feeling gorgeous. Breathe.

4. Imagine yourself back at home now preparing for a date and adorning a similar style or outfit, hair and accessories that you were wearing on your holiday. Notice the detail.

5. Imagine looking at a full-length mirror, dressed and ready for your dream date. Imagine your inner goddess oozing from within and rising out in all her glory, gently trickling down all over your body and your dream date outfit.

6. What is your inner goddess like? Sexy, smart, funny, introspective, chatty, observational? Whatever she is, she is YOU in ALL YOUR GLORY!

7. Imagine taking one final look at yourself in the mirror in your fabulous new outfit, inner goddess radiating from within, all the way out.

8. Next time you go out on a date, wear *this* outfit *and* your inner goddess.

Your state of mind at the beginning of the day has a lot to do with how your day turns out overall.

Guess what! . . . You can *choose* how your day goes, *before* you have it.

This super quick meditation will help get you focused on your desired mood and outcome for the day ahead.

Tip!

If at any stage your day turns pear-shaped (and let's face it, there are those days that do!), return to this ritual and spend a minute or so reconnecting with this meditation experience.

**breathe in your
ideal day**

meditation

1. Sit in an upright and comfortable position on your bed or a quiet, uninterrupted space.
2. Close your eyes and do the *'Belly Breath Meditation'* for a minute or so.
3. Imagine you are in a picture of nature now, anywhere in the world. It could be the beach, a mountain, lush garden, island retreat, or countryside. Anywhere. You choose.
4. Allow all of your senses to come alive. Take in the sights, smells, tastes, sounds and touch sensations around you.
5. Imagine you are sitting in this picture of nature now, meditating and focused on your breath.
6. Ask the question, 'WHAT WORD WILL DESCRIBE MY DAY TODAY?' Happy, productive, thoughtful, grateful, sexy, introspective, relaxing, mindful? Whatever it is, *that* is your word and focus for the day ahead. Choose one.
7. Allow the word to connect with all of your senses now. Breathe. Feel what this word represents in every fibre of your being. Breathe.
8. When you feel ready, open your eyes and gently begin your day, using this word and state of being to set your tone and mood for the day overall.

healthy healing

Safe sun exposure in the fresh outdoors is wonderful for healing and nurturing your body. But when you are unwell and unable to get outside, a great alternative is to nourish yourself through a sun filled meditation exercise.

Whether you are feeling blue or sick with the flu, the *'Healthy Healing Meditation'* is a relaxing way to lift your spirits and nurture your body from the inside out.

warm from the inside out

meditation

1. In a comfortable and quiet spot (feel free to lie down), close your eyes and take a few deep breaths in and out. Let yourself become more relaxed with each new breath. Acknowledge any thoughts or feelings you may have. Let them go as you breathe out.

2. Imagine you are in a beautiful garden now surrounded by lush green grass, flowers and trees. There is a comfortable daybed in the middle of the garden, inviting you to recline on it.

3. Imagine you are now resting on this daybed. Give yourself whatever accessories you need to get comfortable (blanket, cushions, etc). As you become more relaxed, imagine the sun gently warming and nourishing you from head to toe.

4. As you breathe in, notice any discomfort you may feel in your body. Focus now on just those areas where you are feeling most unwell or in pain. Imagine fully breathing the sun in to those areas now. On each new breath out, release the discomfort. On each new breath in, replace it with warm nourished sun filled comfort.

5. When you have breathed in the sun through to your entire body continue laying on your daybed, utterly comforted by this beautiful warm setting.

6. As you near the end of the meditation, you may choose to drift off to sleep or enjoy a deep rest.

7. Finally, when you feel ready, gently open your eyes and slowly stretch, taking care to become present to your body and surroundings.

intention list

Sometimes we over complicate things when we are overloaded. We can feel so overwhelmed with everything we have to do, yet waste so much time wondering and worrying how we are ever going to get it all done.

The to do list is an oldie but a goodie! A tried and tested, simplified method, to get our tasks done. When we take the time to make a to do list, this not only focuses our mind and our time, but it also allows us to feel a sense of accomplishment when we fulfil our to do list at the end of each day!

Use the *'Intention List Meditation'* as a way to switch from worrying about your day ahead to driving your day ahead.

Keep it simple. Seriously . . . simple is good!

Tip!
Don't give yourself a hard time if you don't get everything done. This meditation is designed to get you focused on what you would love to achieve each day. On the flip side, if you *do* get everything done, don't feel you have to add to your list that day. Perhaps give yourself the rest of the day off (now wouldn't that be liberating!)

focus on what's
important

meditation

1. Ensure you have paper and pen close by, then close your eyes and focus on your breath.
2. Turn your attention to your day ahead now. Just imagine your day playing out in your imagination. Notice the detail.
3. Connect to what's important. Meetings, deadlines and so forth. Notice anything else now that you would love to experience today. Include essential items as well as feel good items.
4. Now open your eyes and create an intention list based on what you experienced, felt and saw in your meditation. It could be anything from phoning that friend you've been meaning to call but never quite get around to it, to filing receipts, to de-cluttering the wardrobe, to researching your next holiday, or planning your pitch to your boss for your next raise.
5. Keep this list with you throughout the day and use it to guide your day. When you get sidetracked or lose focus, redirect your attention to your intentions for the day.
6. In addition, notice the fulfilment you feel throughout the day in having completed and ticked off each item on your list.

life purpose

If you don't pursue what you love in life, it usually shows up in other ways throughout your life.

Everyone has a purpose and a reason for being. But life isn't just about having only *one* thing to do and be for the rest of your life. It's also about giving your life meaning and purpose through experiencing *all* of the things you love to do.

Use the *'Life Purpose Meditation'* to discover and reconnect with the way you would most love to spend your time and energy each day, week, month, year.

my reason for being

meditation

1. Ensure you have paper and pen nearby. Begin with the *'Belly Breath Meditation'* to centre yourself and become more relaxed. When you feel ready, imagine yourself now in a picture of nature. Breathe in. Breathe out.

2. Now imagine an image of you from your childhood happy and carefree doing something you loved to do when you were a child.

3. Imagine the little girl you, placing an enormous piece of cardboard in front of her along with coloured pencils and crayons. Ask her to write and draw all of the things she loves to do. Then ask her to sit back and look at the cardboard filled with the things she loves most. Allow this to fill you with happiness and warmth in your heart.

4. Now imagine an image of you as a teenager, placing the same enormous piece of cardboard in front of you along with coloured pencils and crayons. Ask the teenage you to write and draw all of the things she loves to do. Now ask her to sit back and look at the cardboard filled with all the things she loved to do as a little girl and a teenager. Allow this to fill you with happiness and warmth in your heart.

5. Now imagine an image of as a young adult, repeating the process of placing the cardboard in front of you and adding to it the things that you most love to do. Observe this collage of thoughts, dreams and feelings on the cardboard. Allow this to fill you with happiness and warmth in your heart.

6. Now imagine the older you, the woman you are today, observing the same piece of cardboard. Add anything else that you love to do on this piece of cardboard. Finally sit back, observe this enormous cardboard filled with everything the little girl you, the teenage you and the woman you, loves to do. Allow this to fill your heart with warmth and love. Breathe.

7. When you feel ready, open your eyes and make notes of the visions you captured on the cardboard during your meditation.

8. Feel free to create your own real life cardboard visual representation of your meditation insights if you wish.

9. Use these notes and this cardboard to remind you of who you are and what makes you feel good. Take steps each day, week and year towards those things that you love to do and experience most. If you discover more things you love, feel free to continue to add things to your *'Life Purpose Meditation'* notes and cardboard.

"Every day spent doing what you don't love, takes time away from doing what you do love."

Alison Nancye

Sometimes life and everything in it just becomes a bit too much.

We can walk around feeling like we are carrying the biggest load and never really sure where to begin in offloading or dealing with any of it.

Use this meditation to help you let go of the load and get clear about what's really important.

let go of the load

meditation

1. When you are feeling overloaded. S.T.O.P. Remove yourself from your current environment. Literally walk outside and change locations.
2. Choose a quiet spot to stand comfortably without being interrupted for a few minutes. Stand with your feet slightly apart and place your arms beside you with your palms facing outward.
3. Close your eyes. Imagine you are standing on a gorgeous green mountain, completely supported by the generous ground underneath your feet.
4. Allow the concerns of your day to form in your mind until you feel very full with these thoughts.
5. Now imagine you have a basket in each hand. Imagine the thoughts that are weighing you down, are now being physically transported into the baskets in your hands. Keep going with this process, one overloaded thought at a time, until your baskets are full.
6. Now imagine letting the baskets go. Literally imagine releasing the baskets from your hands and all of the items, tasks and responsibilities being released with the baskets.
7. Stand with your arms open wide now. Free of the baskets. Free of the burdens. Free of the load. Breathe.
8. Tilt your head upwards and imagine the sun shining down on you and warming you from the inside out. Breathe.
9. When you feel ready, open your eyes and gently move on with your day.

mind unwind

Apparently the human brain produces approximately 70,000 thoughts per day. How any woman is supposed to offload those thoughts before her head hits the pillow is an exhausting task just *thinking* about it, let alone actually *doing* it!

A good way to get a head start before you turn in for the night is to offload your thoughts at various intervals throughout the day.

But if time gets away from you and your head is chock-a-block full of thoughts when you go to bed, the *'Mind Unwind Meditation'* is a simple way to de-clutter your mind and prepare yourself for a relaxing night's sleep.

Tip!

If you repeat the same track for (say) 30 days at a time, you are less likely to waste time or energy selecting music each night and have more time to meditate.

prepare for a restful
sleep

meditation

1. Choose a music track that makes you feel relaxed and chilled when you listen to it.
2. Dim the lights. Get comfy in bed or in a quiet and warm spot at home.
3. Play the track of your choice and then close your eyes. Turn your attention to the music. Breathe.
4. Move your attention to your belly now. Notice the natural rise and fall of your breath.
5. Simply allow your belly to rise and fall in its own natural way as you continue to listen to your music.
6. Breathe in. Breathe out. Allow your breathing to become deeper as your body becomes more relaxed with each new breath.
7. When the music stops, you can continue listening to soothing tracks while you focus on your breath or gently drift off to sleep.

mini break

If you work at a desk, use a computer or sit in the same position for the best part of the day, you need to take a break. Not just a lunch break, but regular breaks throughout the day.

Your body and mind becomes more restricted and tense as the day goes on. Therefore, it's vitally important to rest your eyes as well as your body and mind. You will feel all the more refreshed for these breaks when you take them.

Give yourself the break it deserves, every day, several times each day.

Tip!
If you wanted to get up from your chair and gently stretch at the end of this *'Mini Break Meditation'* by all means do so. Remember to replenish yourself with H2O breaks as well!

take regular breaks
each day

Alison Nancye

meditation

1. Stop what you are doing at work right now for a minute or two and sit up straight.
2. Close your eyes and focus on the rise and fall of your belly for several seconds.
3. Open your eyes again and look well beyond your current perspective. Choose a totally different spot in your work environment to gaze at.
4. Stare at this spot for several seconds, observing the natural rise and fall of your breath.
5. Close your eyes tightly now. Hold for three seconds and release. Repeat this several times.
6. Close your eyes again and return your attention to your breath.
7. When you feel ready, gently open your eyes and resume your work until your next mini break.

ocean gazing

The ocean is a magnificent place to de-stress, unwind and relax your mind, whether you are listening to it, swimming in it or leisurely gazing at it.

This is a meditation experience you can do with your eyes opened, yet still feel relaxed and centred as a result.

eyes opened meditation

meditation

1. Sit yourself down in view of the ocean and get comfortable.
2. Take in the vast ocean before your eyes.
3. Focus now on one section of the ocean. It could be a wave, the shoreline, ripples washing up near the rocks. Whatever it is, allow yourself to connect with one small part of the magnificent ocean in front of you.
4. Connect with the natural rhythms and movements of this section of the ocean.
5. Allow your breath and the natural rise and fall of your belly to become one with the natural rhythms of the ocean.
6. Take as long as you like to sit, stare and breathe.

There are those days when you are literally running from one thing to the next and if you stop you will not get it all done.

I know those days! I know that life! But if you don't take the time to P.A.U.S.E. between each new activity, you are not giving yourself the opportunity to be fully present and ready to go to the next one.

This technique is seriously simple (and it should be—because let's face it, who has time to add one more thing to their to do list!)

press pause on your day

meditation

1. Do this meditation process at the end of one activity and before beginning another one.
2. Before you launch into your next activity (meeting, supermarket, catch-up with a friend, job interview, bank), whatever it is. S.T.O.P! Literally and physically S.T.O.P. Press the P.AU.S.E. button on your day.
3. Sitting or standing, breathe in and out three times, taking three seconds to breathe in and three seconds to breathe out each time. Do this three times, focussing purely on your breath and the process of the breath going in and out.
4. Next, say either out loud or to yourself "BREATHE. PRESENT. NOW". Repeat these three words, three times.
5. Take one last breath in and out, counting three seconds in and out.
6. Now, step into the next activity of your day, remembering to repeat this process at certain P.AU.S.E. intervals throughout the remainder of your day.

shower cleanse

It's amazing how simple and profound a shower can be at the end of a long hard day.

Being able to literally wash away any stress or concerns from your day, free to step into the next phase of your day, can have a significant impact on your wellbeing overall.

Dedicating this time to let go of your day will help to prepare you to be fully present and ready to step into the next part of your day or evening. It will also prepare you for a restful night's sleep.

release your day

Alison Nancye

meditation

1. Choose a relaxing essential oil. Turn on your shower and allow the bathroom to get steamy.

2. As you remove your clothes, imagine each layer of clothing representing a layer of your day. Any thoughts or feelings weighing you down, anything that made you feel overloaded; literally let it go as you strip away the clothes.

3. Once you are fully undressed, stand directly under the showerhead. Allow the warm water to tumble all the way down your body. Place several drops of your selected essential oil into the steamy shower now. Inhale deeply. Breathe in. Breathe out.

4. Close your eyes for a few moments and imagine the water washing away your day.

5. Open your eyes now and begin gently and slowly washing your hair and body. As you do, imagine you are literally washing away any unwanted residue from your day.

6. Close your eyes at intervals, releasing more of your day under the warm shower. Rinse away now any final unwanted residue.

7. When you feel fully cleansed, complete your shower and prepare yourself for bed or your desired evening ritual.

8. Dab a few drops of your essential oil on to your palms and massage your hands and fingers. Then close your eyes, and breathe in the scent of the oil. Finish by focussing on the natural rise and fall of your belly for as long as you desire.

walking release

For those moments when it all becomes a bit too hard. When you feel frustrated, angry, annoyed and just arghhhhh! When you feel like everyone and everything around you (including the universe!) is working against you, use the *'Walking Release Meditation'*.

The thing is, the more you stay in that space of anxious energy, the more you feed it. You actually need to leave the space you are in and literally walk outside and physically let it go.

Instead of putting your energy *into* the anger put your energy into *releasing* the anger.

walk it out

Alison Nancye

meditation

1. When you feel that nothing is going your way or everything and everyone is working against you, put on your walking or running shoes, grab your iPod and head out the door. Select music that is uplifting and energising.

2. Begin walking. Start to pound that pavement, music playing in your ears in the background.

3. Choose to let go of the thoughts and feelings you may have about others or whatever is upsetting you. Just choose to forget about it for now.

4. As you walk, allow your strides to become stronger and more powerful as you lose yourself in the music. It's as if you are walking to the beat of the music, dancing down the street and singing along internally to yourself. Everything and everyone else forgotten. Just you, the music and the beat of your feet pounding the pavement.

5. If you can walk to nature, especially water (very calming) great. If not, keep walking anyway. Walk, breathe and release for as long as you need.

6. Before ending your walk, choose a quiet spot to sit. Either change the track on your iPod to something soothing or turn the music off altogether. Use this time to sit, breathe and rest your eyes. (Use the steps to the *'Belly Breath Meditation'* here if you like).

7. When you feel ready, prepare for the walk home. Choose whatever album or track on your iPod you enjoy.

Alison Nancye is an author and speaker of lifestyle, wellbeing, inspirational, and meditation content.

Alison is the author of the recipe-style life-mentoring book 'RECIPES FOR EVERYDAY LIFE'—create the life of your dreams. She was commissioned to write the handbook 'PLANNING A CAREER CHANGE' and is soon releasing her first novel 'NOTE TO SELF'—a woman's journey to getting a life. Alison is the co-creator of the 'UMBRELLA GIRLS' series of inspirational picture books for girls, including authoring the soon to be released 'THE WISDOM OFFICE.'

Alison's media profile includes editorial contributions featured in Australian teen publication DOLLY Magazine and popular Australian lifestyle and wellbeing magazines such as INSIGHT, DUMBO FEATHER and EMPOWER. Television appearances include a Regular Guest role on Australia's CHANNEL 9 'Mornings with Kerri-Anne' and CLINIQUE TV sharing life dreams, wellness and meditation content. Alison has also been a guest on Byron Bay's BAY FM Radio.

Her articles, editorial, blogs and tips are featured online in places such as MOTHERINC, PLAYGROUP NSW INC, SHESAID, and WEALTH ADVISOR.

author

This **HANDBAG MEDITATIONS for WOMEN** book is part of a series of books Alison has created for women, girls, teens, mums and grandmas.

Alison has been meditating for over 15 years and uses it in her daily life in everything from cooking up the family dinner menu for the month ahead, to manifesting her dreams each day, week and year. She used meditation leading up to and during the birth of her two children, as well as imagining and dreaming on her wedding ceremony and celebrations. Alison uses meditation for content, clarity and creativity when writing her books and even used meditation to dream on and manifest finding her dad almost 10 years ago, after a lifetime of never knowing him.

Alison Nancye lives in Sydney, Australia and regularly travels to the United States for work. She is married to Cinematographer Francesco Biffone and they have two children Bellina and Benicio.

"Everyone can meditate. Everyone can dream. It is the practise of doing so that makes the difference to your reality in the end."

Alison Nancye